HOW CAN WE
LIVE OUR FAITH
FROM THE INSIDE OUT?

MICHAEL P. V. BARRETT

REFORMATION HERITAGE BOOKS
GRAND RAPIDS, MICHIGAN

Reformation Heritage Books
2965 Leonard St. NE
Grand Rapids, MI 49525
616-977-0889
orders@heritagebooks.org
www.heritagebooks.org

Printed in the United States of America
18 19 20 21 22 23/10 9 8 7 6 5 4 3 2 1

ISBN 978-1-60178-640-1
ISBN 978-1-60178-641-8 (e-pub)

For additional Reformed literature, request a free book list from Reformation Heritage Books at the above regular or e-mail address.

HOW CAN WE
LIVE OUR FAITH
FROM THE INSIDE OUT?

———————— ✕ ————————

Many Christians have a problem with the Christian life. Faith loses its attractiveness. Initial enthusiasm dwindles, and disillusionment sets in. For some people, Christianity is just a set of beliefs, and for others a rigid set of standards. Nearly every new emerging movement or seminar for success is an effort to capitalize on the dissatisfaction of Christians who have somehow failed to understand what the Bible says about the Christian life. There is a practical side to doctrine; Scripture inseparably links believing and living.

It is amazing that the truths which so over-whelmed the thinking of first-century Christians rarely seem to cross the minds of twenty-first-century believers. In the gospel there is a dynamic to energize and guide life along the proper paths. Only when Christians ignore the gospel, and the beauty of the Savior that lies at its heart, do they find Christianity to be drudgery. Too often people reduce belief in the gospel to a past decision rather than elevating and centralizing it into a corpus of truths that are the constant object of present faith and application. All of life for the Christian ought to be squarely focused on Christ. Christ, His cross, and the completeness of His gospel must interfere with life; He must be the focal point for living out our faith. He must stand in the way of every sin and point the way to piety. It is always the case that right thinking about the gospel produces right living under the gospel.

Colossians 3:1–17 makes this connection clearly. In Colossians 2, Paul exposed and warned against all the additions to Christ that were supposed to lead to spiritual attainment and satisfaction. He does so first by expounding the completeness of Christ in terms of His deity and humanity (v. 9) and then the believer's completeness in Him in terms of union (v. 10). Significantly, the words "fulness" and "complete" are from the same Greek root. Paul's play on words underscores the wonder of the truth itself. Our completeness is in union with Christ, not in how we adhere to religious rituals or other manifestations of "will worship" (v. 23). In Colossians 3, he builds on the theology of throne union with Christ and looks at the Christian's life from two perspectives— inside and outside. The apostle defines the principles for Christian living and then the procedure for living the Christian life. This text is a classic example of how deep theology translates into the practices of life. The passage begins in the lofty environs of heaven and transitions to the lowly arena of daily living. The logic is clear in proving once again that we are complete in Christ. In Colossians 3 we see that there are two perspectives: the principle for Christian living and the procedures for Christian living—the hidden life and the seen life.

THE PRINCIPLE: THE HIDDEN LIFE

In Colossians 3:1–4, Paul expounds the theology that is essential and foundational to both spiritual life and godly living. He draws our attention to the objective realities of the believer's union with Christ with all of its representative, vital, intimate, and mystical significance. This union is equally true for every genuine believer in Jesus Christ, but is not equally enjoyed or consciously experienced by all. Hence, he directs us how to think in the light of the facts. Three thoughts stand out about the believer's hidden life.

The Fact of the Hidden Life

Verse 3 declares the proposition, "For ye are dead, and your life is hid with Christ in God." This is indisputable fact. The text more literally reads, "You died." Since Paul is writing to those who were very much alive physically, this past death refers to something spiritual—even mystical. Don't be afraid of this word. Theologically, it refers to spiritual truth that surpasses human comprehension because of the transcendence of its nature and significance. It is a most appropriate word to designate the believer's union with Jesus Christ, a truth that, notwithstanding its reality, defies full explanation. The statement "You died," then, takes us to that mysterious and mystical union of every believer with Jesus Christ in His death on the cross and in all other aspects of His work. There is a sense, though incomprehensible, in which every believer jointly participates and shares in the work of the Lord Jesus. This staggers the mind. Consider these astounding statements that declare the believer's communion with the death of Christ: "I am crucified with Christ" (Gal. 2:20). "We are buried with him by baptism into death" (Rom. 6:4; see also Col. 2:12). "Our old man is crucified with him" (Rom. 6:6). "If one died for all, then were all dead" (i.e., all for whom He died, died) (2 Cor. 5:14). Obviously we did not hang on the cross along with Christ to suffer all the physical agony and torment that He endured in both body and soul. In the physical sense, Christ suffered and died alone as the substitute for His people. He bore our penalty and exempted us from ever having to pay the penalty of our sin. He is our federal, or representative, head who stands in our place; and we were, thus, united to Him through faith in Him. When Christ died, all His people died with Him. God regarded believers—His elect and Christ's inheritance—as being in His Son.

On the cross satisfaction against our sin was secured, and our connection to the power of sin was severed. Being crucified with Christ means that we should look down on sin and the old life from that vantage point. Sin that is so alluring to our worldly eyes loses its appeal when viewed from the old rugged cross.

Ironically, although we died, we live in another sense. Our life has been "hid with Christ in God." This mystical death to sin did not produce a lifeless corpse. On the contrary, union with Christ's death always includes union with His resurrection and life (Romans 6). Consider verse 1, which assumes that believers were raised with Christ. Community with His death always includes community with His life. Significantly, Paul uses a different verb form to express the hidden life. Whereas we died once for all, the form of the verb "hid" addresses both the past act of being hidden and its continuing consequences. When we died with Christ, we were at that time raised with Him and our lives were hidden in Him, and there we constantly remain. Given where Christ is sitting at the right hand of God (3:1), this is all the more remarkable. He is in heaven; we are in heaven in Him (Eph. 2:6). This is why I use the expression "throne union" to refer to the believer being enthroned with Christ in heaven. By faith we are to know and reckon for ourselves that we are alive in Him (Rom. 6:11). The implications and applications of this throne union are far-reaching, both regarding our security with God and our duty in the world. The world can't see us there (after all, our lives are hidden with God in Christ), but God does so because all things are open before His eyes (Heb. 4:13). The Head-body analogy is one way Paul describes union with Christ (Col. 1:18). It is our security that God sees the body through the Head; it is our duty that the world should see the Head through the body. It is sobering to realize that the world's estimation of the Head is so often determined by what they perceive about the body. This makes a huge difference in how we live out our faith.

The Imperatives of the Hidden Life
Paul issues two imperatives in verses 1 and 2 that are the logical corollaries to his proposition regarding the believer's union with Christ. The logic is clear from the opening statement that assumes the reality of fact: "You have been raised with Christ." Given the fact of life union with Jesus Christ, there are some key things that we should think about in light of this reality. Both imperatives, "seek" (v. 1) and "set your affection" (v. 2), involve thinking. Imperatives are always addressed to the will and identify what we are obliged to do.

First, *be seeking the things above* (v. 1). The form of the verb demands a continuing and habitual process. This is not to be an occasional thought, but one that becomes regular routine. This is essentially a process of Christian meditation. Furthermore, this seeking does not refer simply to an investigation but includes the thoroughgoing effort to obtain what is sought. The direction of this ongoing effort is above, where Christ sits exalted in His session at the Father's right hand. This apostolic advice parallels the words of Christ Himself in His discourse on the mount, admonishing us to lay up treasures in heaven and not on earth because "where your treasure is, there will your heart be also" (Matt. 6:19–21). There is no treasure more valuable than Jesus, who is the pearl of great price. Nothing else approaches His infinite value and intrinsic worth. To regard Him so is to have our earthly hearts fixed where He is and where we are in union with Him. Again, this seeking is more than just an examination of doctrine; it is a striving to experience and possess the fullness of the blessings that flow from biblical truth. Too often Christians are like the ten spies who admired and could describe the grapes of Canaan but who failed to possess them; they remained on the border of blessing. Examining and expounding gospel truth is fundamental, but it is vital that we go beyond its exposition to its experience. We must live in the reality of what we believe. Let us not live on the border of spiritual blessing, but let us enter its fullness. Let us be like Caleb and Joshua who entered into the possession of what God had promised and provided.

Second, *set your affection on things above*: literally, "be thinking about the above things" (v. 2). The form of this verb also demands continuing and habitual activity. Thinking is the exercise of the mind, and it is spiritually crucial. Paul uses the noun form of this verb in Romans 8:6 where he says, "To be carnally minded is death; but to be spiritually minded is life and peace." People's mind-sets are litmus tests revealing who they really are. Thinking is the first step to doing. Right thinking and right believing produce right behavior. It is imperative that believers, therefore, habitually and routinely engage their minds on the above things where Christ is and where they are with Christ, who is seated on His throne. I don't know how thinking works, but I know it works. I know that when you think about something hard enough and long enough, you can't stop thinking about it. The issue is what we think about when we're not thinking! It is as though habitual thinking wears grooves in the brain. Consider Philippians 4:8, where Paul lists the characteristics of some of the above things that we should think about. We need to "groove our brains" with things that are true, honest, just, pure, lovely, of good report, virtuous, and praiseworthy—all of which are subsumed in Christ Himself.

This obviously does not mean that we never think about other things, for other things are unavoidable parts of life. Yet it does mean that all we think about and all that we do are governed by the fact that we are united to Christ. Thinking about this union with Christ affects everything else in our lives. Contrary to the common adage that someone can be so heavenly minded so as to be of no earthly good, the gospel logic is that the more heavenly minded we are, the more earthly good we will be able to do.

The Prospect of the Hidden Life

The prospect of the hidden life is that it will not remain hidden. A day is coming when faith transitions to sight, when the invisible becomes visible, and when our subjective experience becomes one with our objective position. The Greek verb translated "appear" in verse 4 means to be manifest, completely revealed and open. Christ, "who is our life" — the essence of the life we possess and the object of our passions — will one day be openly revealed in all of His splendid glory (v. 4). Adding to the wonder of these truths is that we will be manifested in glory with Him. There is no separating Christ and His people, not in heaven and not now. The prospect of that certain glory shared with Christ puts all the stuff of time in its proper place. Occupation with Christ is the secret to everything in the Christian life. So living out our faith means that we live now with a view to then.

THE PROCEDURE: THE SEEN LIFE

What is true on the inside will show itself on the outside. Although our union with Christ is hidden from view, the evidences of that union should be seen. Doctrine breeds duty. Ethical demands flow from theological truths. Simply said, union with Christ looks like something. In Colossians 3:5–17, the apostle details the implications of being in Christ both in negative and in positive terms. His logic was adopted by the Westminster divines in their classic definition of sanctification as "the work of God's free grace whereby we are renewed in the whole man after the image of God and are enabled more and more to die unto sin and to live unto righteousness" (Westminster Shorter Catechism 35). We should follow this logic as well as we consider how the hidden life reveals itself.

Death to Sin

In verses 5–11, the focus is on the negative component of sanctification, which is death to sin. Believers are to put off the vices belonging to the old life outside of Christ. It only makes sense that if we died judicially to sin in union with Christ in His death on the cross, then we should also die practically to sin as we live in union with His life through union with Him in His resurrection. Here is how Paul put it in Romans 6:4: "Therefore we are buried with him by baptism into death: that like as Christ was raised up from the dead by the glory of the Father, even so we also should walk in newness of life." Paul's imagery here is suggestive. In physical burial, the corrupting corpse is separated from the land of the living. In remarkable irony, in this spiritual burial with Christ, the "living" corpse of the believer is separated from the corruption of the world. Paul's argument in Colossians 3:5–11 suggests three thoughts.

First, Paul demands *the duty of dying*. He issues commands; therefore, these are not simply apostolic or pastoral suggestions for optional behavior, but imperatives that demand obedience. We are to *mortify* our earthly members along with their sinful practices (v. 5). The word "members" usually designates physical limbs or body parts, but by metonymical extension it here includes whatever is in us that is of this world and bent to sin. We must not permit our physical bodies or anything concerning us to continue to be instruments of sin. This idea parallels what Paul calls the "old man," which we will consider in a moment. In many ways, the biggest threat to our sanctification is ourselves. Therefore, we must die to self. But this death is not by natural causes, for dying to self is most unnatural for sinners. The word "mortify," perhaps, has lost some of its shock value in modern use. The word means to kill, with all its violent connotations. Killing sin is godly suicide, in a sense. We must kill self, put it to death. The language is blunt, forceful, and a bit shocking, but no more so than Christ's counsel to eliminate offending body parts for the spiritual welfare of the soul (Matt. 5:29–30). This member-killing refers to an urgent and immediate effort to eliminate by execution everything that is at odds with God. If our life is truly in heaven, then we must kill off the sinful stuff of our earthly existence. The consequence of Christ's dying for us and our dying in Him is that we should not live anymore with a view to ourselves—our interests, ambitions, or desires that would be contrary to grace (see 2 Cor. 5:15).

We are also *to put off sinful practices* (Col. 3:8), which are like things that stain and ruin the appearance of a garment. The imagery changes here, but the topic is the same. By using an illustration about changing clothes, Paul makes the point clear that life in Christ cannot look the same as life did before. It is only logical that after a bath, you would not put on the filthy clothes that made the bath necessary to begin with. So spiritually, after the washing of regeneration, we must put off the garments that have been mucked up from the dirt of this world. Life in union with Christ requires a visible transformation. The Bible knows nothing about a gospel that makes no demands on life or requires no changes. Grace finds sinners in the most indescribable filth, but grace never leaves sinners where it finds them.

Second, Paul identifies *the sins subject to death*. He gives two extensive, though not exhaustive, lists of sins to illustrate the kind of behavior that is incongruous to the hidden life in Christ (vv. 5, 8). It is not my intent to define or elaborate on each of these specified vices, but I want us to grasp the principal point the apostle is making. Each group lists five sins, all of which relate to specific violations of the second division of God's moral law, which deals with people's relationship to other people. Transgressing the second division of the law is evidence of transgressing the first division. People's relationship with their fellows is a mirror of their relationship with God. In verse 5, the sins listed progress from outward acts to inward attitudes, whereas in verse 8 the sins described move from inward attitudes to outward acts. Putting the two groups together creates a logical *chiasmus* in which the center focus is on the inward attitudes and thoughts. *Chiasmus* is a common Hebraic literary structure throughout the Bible. It's a different logic than modern Westerners are accustomed to using, but recognizing it often helps us follow the progression of biblical arguments. It is like a big X that draws attention to where the lines intersect. So here at the point of intersection are the sins of the mind. This focus affirms our proposition that thinking determines behavior. Sins in the head are no less serious than sins of the hands.

Another literary technique is also operating when all ten sins are combined. It would be a mistake to assume that these specifically designated sins are the only ones with which we must be concerned. Here Paul employs a device called *brachylogy*, which is a partial list of something to indicate the totality of something. He gives us similar lists elsewhere (e.g., 1 Cor. 6:9–10; Gal. 5:19–21). Paul's point, therefore, is not just that we should deal with these sins specifically but with sin generally. This is a representative list to include all vices that are contrary to holiness. The list of sins to which you may be particularly susceptible may differ from mine, but the text makes it clear that we must deal directly with the sins in our lives no matter what they are.

Verse 7 gives hope that we can indeed mortify and put off our sins. There is power in the gospel to enable the transformation that grace requires. The Colossian believers used to walk and live within the sphere of those sins, but now they don't. What used to characterize their lives no longer does so. This reversal of lifestyle marks every genuine believer. No Christians are experientially as holy as they should be nor as holy as they will be when they appear with Christ in glory, but neither are they as unholy as they were. Every saint can affirm John Newton's often quoted testimony, "I am not what I ought to be, I am not what I want to be, I am not what I hope to be in another world; but still I am not what I once used to be, and by the grace of God I am what I am."

Third, Paul explains *the reasons for death to sin*. He gives two reasons, one negative and one positive. Negatively, death to sin is necessary because sin angers God (v. 6). Every sin is a violation of His righteous justice, and His wrath is poised against it (Rom. 1:18). Whereas the sinful world stands already condemned, all those in Christ have been delivered from condemnation (Rom. 5:1). Insofar as Christians, then, are no longer under God's wrath, sinfulness should no longer dominate their practices. We are no longer subject to God's wrath due to Christ's atoning work. The cross stands as the greatest evidence of God's justice and wrath against sin. God put Christ on the cross in our place for our sins, and so must we take up the cross and follow Christ. It was because of our sin that Christ died. To think of why He died and to remember that we died in union with Him is reason enough to press us to die to sin.

Positively, death to sin is necessary because we have been restored in the image of God (vv. 9–10). Paul transitions to this argument by linking two phrases ("put off" and "put on") to the imperative "Lie not one to another," suggesting that wearing the wrong thing can be deceptive. While I don't think it is true that clothes make the person, they do reveal something about the person. I love to wear camouflage. So when I wear it along with a hat with a deer or turkey logo, you would be safe to assume that I hunt and that I wish I were in the woods where neither you nor the "critters" could see me. On the other hand, if I were to wear the scrubs of a surgeon, that would be misleading and potentially dangerous if you believed what you saw. The point very simply is that you should dress according to what you are. To be hidden in union with Christ demands death to sin because we have put off the old man and put on the new.

In his commentary on Colossians 3:9, Calvin defines the "old man" as "whatever we bring from our mother's womb, and whatever we are by nature." In this context, the "old man" designates the unregenerate state, in which there is no spiritual life or sensitivity and no impulse toward God or spiritual things. It is this sinful nature that gives rise and expression to every evil deed. The simple fact is that those who trust Christ don't wear those clothes any more. No longer are they spiritually dead, insensitive, or motionless toward God. They look different because they have put on the new man. The "new man" refers to the regenerate nature in which the Holy Spirit has implanted the principle of spiritual life in us. This is the new garment worn by everyone hidden in Christ. Paul describes the new man as being continually, habitually, progressively renewed in the knowledge of the Creator's image. Much like our death to sin, we both have been renewed in knowledge after the image of Him who created us, and we are being renewed continually in His image in Christ. We are not yet sinless, but we want to be, and we are headed in that direction. It is beyond the scope of our meditation here to think about the full meaning and many implications of the image of God. Suffice it to say that it was the unique mark of humanity's original creation that was tragically marred by the fall into sin and wonderfully restored by God's grace through the gospel. Jesus Christ is the ideal image, even the perfect manifestation of God (Col. 1:15), and it is only through Him and in Him that we are being renewed in God's image. Christ, the second Adam, reversed the curse and restored everything lost by the first Adam. This includes the true knowledge of the true God, as well as righteousness and holiness (Eph. 4:24).

Regardless of race or nationality (Col. 3:11), all believers will look the same in this regard: they have all put on the new man. To put on the new man is to be adorned with Christ, who is all and in all: He is our uniform. Christ is everything in the realm of grace; there is no experience or enjoyment of grace without Him. We die to sin by looking to Christ. As we look, we are changed progressively from glory to glory (2 Cor. 3:18) until He appears, when we will be like Him because we will see Him as He is (1 John 3:2). If seeing Christ with our eyes is how glorification works, then it follows that seeing Christ with the eyes of faith is how sanctification works. There is something about seeing Jesus that makes us like Him.

Alive to Righteousness
Living out our faith is more than not doing bad things; it involves doing good things as well. A life of faith is not just negative; it is most positive. Again the Westminster Shorter Catechism says it well that in our sanctification we are enabled to "live more and more unto righteousness." Paul concludes his argument about the "seen life" by expounding what it is to live spiritually (Col. 3:12–17). There are three points to his exposition.

First, he delineates the *marks of spiritual life*. He continues the clothes analogy with the imperative "put on" and then lists the virtues that are to be seen in the new man, the style of clothing to wear. He addresses the imperative to those who are chosen by God, who are set apart as distinct, and who are the objects of fixed and continuing love, which are other ways of identifying those whose lives have been hidden with Christ in God. Again, it is not my intent to define each of the virtues, all of which follow the same pattern as the list of vices by relating to the second division of the law. I want simply to draw some conclusions from this list. Significantly, all the virtues included are characteristics of Christ Himself. That should not be surprising since Christ-likeness is the ultimate objective of our salvation: God has predestinated us to be conformed to the image of His Son (Rom. 8:29). So to put on bowels of mercies is to be like Christ, and so it is right down the list. Paul explicitly makes this connection when he sets Christ as the pattern for forgiveness: "as Christ forgave you, so also do ye" (v. 13). It is noteworthy that Paul isolates love as the bond, or belt, that keeps everything complete and together (v. 14). The essence of this love is selflessness, and who more perfectly than Christ evidenced this selfless love, climaxing in giving Himself for His church (Eph. 5:25)? There is nothing that will spoil, spot, and stain the Christian's wardrobe more than self. Be like Christ by putting on godly virtue.

I would suggest also that in this list of virtues, Paul is employing the same literary device of brachylogy that he used to list all the vices. These are representative virtues that imply every conceivable virtue that conforms to and expresses obedience to God's standard of righteousness, namely, His law and His Son. Remember that what the world sees in us determines what it will think of Christ. Ironically, as God sees the church as the body in Christ the Head, so the world sees Christ the Head through us as His body. This is a sobering thought that should dictate our actions.

Second, he details the *method of spiritual life* (vv. 15–16). Paul issues three imperatives to explain how to live out our faith; all are in a form that expresses constant and habitual activity, underscoring that living the Christian life is a full-time occupation.

The first and third imperatives express tolerative ideas: "Let the peace of God rule," and "Let the word of Christ dwell." This is what should happen, and we should do what is necessary to allow it to happen. The peace that comes only from God must rule in our hearts—our inner being where we think and feel— and it must determine our actions. Although this peace could refer to the subjective peace of soul that comes from God evidenced by assurance of faith, confidence in forgiveness, and contentment, I'm more inclined to understand it as the objective peace of reconciliation that Christ accomplished through His blood (Col. 1:20; see also Eph. 2:14). In a real sense, the peace of God is summed up in Christ. That may account for the textual variant adopted in some versions that reads "the peace of Christ." So much in the text has focused on Christ's death and what we should think about it that it makes sense the reconciliation between God and us that is ours through His blood should factor into our relationship to His body. The word "rule" is an athletic term meaning to act as an umpire, to arbitrate disputes, or to make the calls. Peace with God will translate to peace within the body of Christ. That will happen when we allow Christ to settle every matter among us.

We should let the word about Christ dwell in us abundantly (v. 16). To put it simply, the gospel should be at home in our hearts, where it will then impact every decision, plan, and activity of life. We are to live within the sphere of God's Word. For this to happen, we must know what Scripture says. *Sola Scriptura* is part of our Reformed tradition, but it must be more than just a component of our creed. Dwelling together implies intimacy, and if we confess love for the Word, it must be more than talk. Paul uses a series of circumstantial participles to express what the indwelling word is going to look like. First, it will affect our conversation with fellow believers (teaching and admonishing one another). Second, it will direct praise to God by singing the new song in our hearts that He has put there by grace by using psalms, hymns, and spiritual songs. Singing praise to Christ because His Word dwells in our hearts edifies other believers as well. This, by the way, reflects a slightly different translation, involving only punctuation. As translated in the Authorized Version, psalms, hymns, and spiritual songs are the means of mutual teaching and admonition. I would prefer translating the verse with a different punctuation, which would more naturally link "with psalms and hymns and spiritual songs" to singing rather than teaching: "Let the word of Christ dwell in you richly, in all wisdom teaching and admonishing one another, with psalms and hymns and spiritual songs singing with grace in your heart to the Lord." But wherever the comma is placed, it is clear that the indwelling word of Christ is going to be seen outwardly. This is the salient point. What is inside shows itself on the outside.

Sandwiched between the two tolerative imperatives is the command "Be ye thankful" (v. 15). Constant and habitual gratitude is a key component of living out our faith. It is a common theme throughout Paul's letters and in his personal testimony. No exposition is required at this point. How can we not be thankful when we think of Christ, His work, and what that means for us personally?

Finally, Paul declares the *motive for spiritual life* (v. 17). Why we do what we do is important; motives matter. For the Christian, Christ's name and glory should be the principal concern in everything thought, said, and done. The Scripture disallows the modern—or perhaps I should say post-modern—notion of compartmentalizing life so that religious life is somehow unrelated to everything else. On the contrary, nothing about life is outside the scope of the relationship we have with Jesus Christ. Who Christ is, His authority over us, our identification with Him, our knowledge of His will, and our thankfulness to God for Him all factor into every sphere of

life. To say what we say and to do what we do consciously and intentionally in the name of Jesus will
unquestionably affect what we say and do in everything. Right thinking produces right behavior. We
can't get away from this axiom.

Living out our faith simply amounts to living in
the reality of the religion we say we believe. There
can be no disconnect between belief and practice,
between doctrine and duty. Objective truth must
transfer to subjective experience. The more we know
the gospel and our completeness in Christ, the
more we can enjoy and experience the gospel in our
lives. Theology is the most practical of disciplines
and sciences. In the head we must know the truth;
in the heart we must believe the truth; with the
hands we must implement and evidence the truth.
Living our faith starts on the inside and shows itself
on the outside.